LAURA K. MURRAY

grow with me

CORN

CREATIVE EDUCATION · CREATIVE PAPERBACKS

Published by Creative Education
and Creative Paperbacks
P.O. Box 227, Mankato, Minnesota 56002
Creative Education and Creative Paperbacks are
imprints of The Creative Company
www.thecreativecompany.us

Design by Ellen Huber
Production by Travis Green
Art direction by Rita Marshall
Printed in Malaysia

Photographs by Alamy (AgStock Images, Inc.),
Corbis (145/Hiroshi Higuchi/Ocean, AgStock
Images, Gerry Ellis/Minden Pictures, Found
Image Press, David Harrigan/ableimages, David
Nunuk/Science Photo Library, Visuals Unlimited),
Dreamstime (roibul, Somchai Somsanitangkul),
Getty Images (Vladimir Vladimirov), Shutterstock
(apisit, Atelier_A, bogdanhoda, DibasUA, EM Arts,
foto76, LENA GABRILOVICH, Brent Hofacker, I love
photo, indigolotos, juniart, Sakdinon Kadchiangsaen,
metalstock, Paladin12, Piyato, rsooll, Rashid Valitov,
Warren Price Photography, xpixel)

Library of Congress Cataloging-in-Publication Data
Murray, Laura K.
Corn / Laura K. Murray.
p. cm. — (Grow with me)
Includes bibliographical references and index.
Summary: An exploration of the life cycle and life span
of corn, using up-close photographs and step-by-step
text to follow a corn plant's growth process from seed to
seedling to mature plant.

ISBN 978-1-60818-561-0 (hardcover)
ISBN 978-1-62832-162-3 (pbk)
1. Corn—Juvenile literature. 2. Corn—Life cycles—
Juvenile literature. I. Title. II. Series: Grow with me.
SB191.M2M88 2015
633.1'5—dc23   2014028005

CCSS: RI.3.1, 2, 3, 4, 5, 6, 7, 8; RI.4.1, 2, 3, 4, 5, 7; RF.3.3, 4

First Edition HC 9 8 7 6 5 4 3 2 1
First Edition PBK 9 8 7 6 5 4 3 2 1

TABLE OF CONTENTS

4 Corn-fed chickens produce eggs with yellower yolks, or middles.

Corn is an important crop to many people and animals. People eat sweet corn and pop-corn. Farmers use field corn to feed **livestock**. They make the grain into cereal, too.

Corn is an annual plant. That means it must be replanted every year. Corn needs **fertile** soil, water, and lots of sunlight. Some people call corn "maize" (*MAZE*).

5

6   *The husk around an ear of corn keeps the kernels inside safe.*

A corn plant has leaves and a thick stalk, or stem. Most stalks are about eight feet (2.4 m) tall. But they can grow much higher! At the top of the stem is a group of flowers. This part is called the tassel.

In the middle of the plant are other flowers called ears. An outer covering called a husk covers each ear. Inside the husk, kernels grow on a cob. Most kernels are white or yellow. Others are blue, purple, or red.

7

kernel

husk leaf

Sweet corn has tender kernels for eating. Other kinds of corn have harder kernels. Field corn is grown to feed animals. It is ground up to make some human foods, too.

Field corn includes dent corn, flour corn, waxy corn, and flint corn. Popcorn is a special type of flint corn. Its hard kernels puff up when heated.

8

Indian corn is a color-ful flint corn used as fall decoration.

9

A kernel is a seed. Corn grows when a person plants a seed in the ground. The temperature of the soil should be at least 55 °F (12.8 °C).

Corn is planted in rows. It grows outdoors in big gardens or fields. Corn requires lots of space. Each day, a corn plant needs 8 to 10 hours of full sunlight. It needs water, too.

10

Corn seeds are usually planted about two inches (5.1 cm) deep.

Farmers plant corn rows 2.5 to 3 feet (76.2–91.4 cm) apart.

11

A corn seed is dry. Inside the seed is an **embryo** (*EM-bree-oh*). The embryo is wrapped in a hard shell called a seed coat. Water softens the seed coat. The seed begins to **germinate** (*JER-mih-nate*).

The embryo bursts through the seed coat. The seed's root reaches down into the soil. It collects water for the plant. After 7 to 21 days, a stem pushes up through the warm ground. The new plant is called a seedling.

12

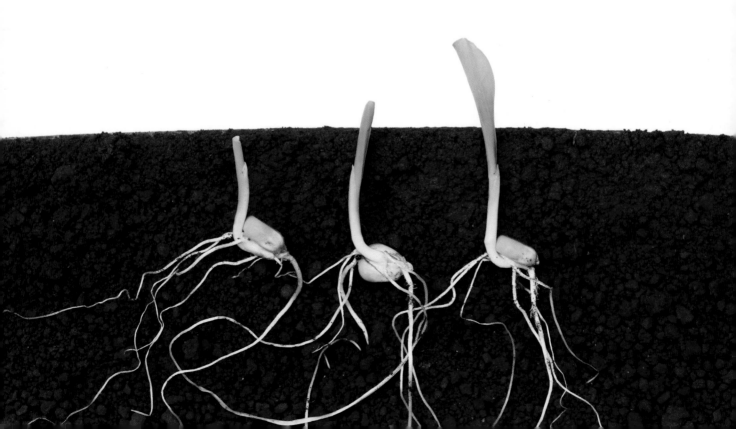

Leaves appear about a week after a seedling first emerges. 13

14 Collars on a corn stalk are used to mark the plant's growth stage.

Warm weather and soil will help seedlings grow faster.

The seedling grows slowly. Its first leaf is called the flag leaf. It has a rounded tip. Every few days, another leaf appears. These new leaves are pointed. They use sunlight, air, and water to make food for the plant. The part where a leaf meets the stalk is called a collar.

Some roots grow above ground to help the stalk stand up. Soon, the flag leaf and old leaves die. As the plant grows, 8 to 10 tiny ear **shoots** grow from the main stalk. Ear shoots are female flowers. One or more shoots will grow into ears of corn.

15

The corn plant reaches its full height about 65 days after coming out of the soil. Its tassel reaches up from the top of the stalk. The tassel is the male flower. It makes **pollen**.

A few days later, long threads called silks come out of the ear shoots. The silks are sticky. They wave in the wind. The wind blows pollen onto the silks. Then the pollen travels into the ear. Each **pollinated** silk will help one kernel grow.

Silks (pictured) grow long to receive the tassel's (opposite) pollen. 17

Older ears of corn have dark yellow kernels and brown silks.

18

Many farmers grow **hybrid** (*HI-brid*) corn. They mix and match different types of corn to produce bigger and better-tasting corn.

Farmers may remove the tassels of some corn plants in a field. That way, only certain plants can pollinate the entire crop.

The tallest sweet corn plant on record was 35.2 feet (10.7 m) high.

19

20 American farms produce about 32 percent of the world's corn.

After pollination, the corn grows quickly. The kernels are small and white at first. But soon they turn yellow and plump. The silks dry, and the tassel turns brown. This is called the milk stage because kernels have a white liquid inside.

Most plants have one or two ears of corn. Ears of sweet corn grow to be about 7 to 10 inches (17.8–25.4 cm) long. An ear has 500 to 1,200 kernels. Sweet corn is ready to be picked 20 days after the silks appear.

21

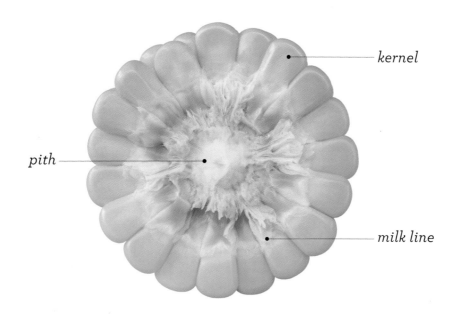

kernel

pith

milk line

Some people **harvest** sweet corn by hand. But farmers use machines called combines to harvest field corn. A combine cuts down the stalks and separates the ears and kernels.

Weeds, bugs, or worms might destroy corn plants. Animals such as birds and deer like to eat corn. Storms and cold can kill corn, too. Many young corn plants get sick with light and dark **smut**. Smut makes it hard for plants to grow.

22

The parts of corn smut that look like mushrooms are called galls.

The header on the front of a combine chops down corn stalks.

23

24 People often add butter and spices to boiled or grilled corn on the cob.

People cook sweet corn to eat it right off the cob. A high amount of sugar in the kernels makes it taste sweet. People eat popped popcorn with butter and salt.

In many countries, dried corn is a basic food called cornmeal. Field corn makes **cornstarch**, oil, and corn syrup. Corn syrup is used in peanut butter, soda, ketchup, and more. Tortillas (*tor-TEE-ahs*) are made from corn, too.

25

Thousands of years ago, people first **cultivated** corn in **Mesoamerica**. The ears of corn were very small. Then American Indians began growing corn crops. After Europeans arrived in the Americas, corn spread around the world.

Today, most corn is harvested as grain. But it can be used in many other things such as glue or fuel. States in the **Corn Belt** grow the most corn in the United States.

The grain left behind after corn is made into fuel is sold for animal feed.

27

Field corn has darker and tougher kernels than sweet corn.

28   If a corn plant is not harvested, it dries out. Its kernels harden and darken. Soon, a black layer forms on the cob. The plant withers and dies. The same plant will not grow again next year. In the spring, a new corn seed will be planted. It will grow tall under the warm sun.

The total growth cycle of most corn takes about 120 days.

A corn seed is planted in spring.

 After 7 to 21 days, the seed germinates.

The seedling emerges from the soil.

Ear shoots appear 30 to 45 days after emergence.

30

Tassels are fully visible about  65 days after emergence.

 Wind carries pollen from the tassels to the silks.

Kernels grow on the cob for about 20 days and reach the milk stage.

After 35 to 45 days, the dry plant forms a black layer on its kernels.

The corn plant dries up and dies.

Corn Belt: *the midwestern region of the United States that grows most of the nation's corn*

cornstarch: *a ground corn flour that is often used in cooking*

crop: *a plant that is grown as food*

cultivated: *planted by people; not wild*

embryo: *the part of a seed that grows into a plant*

fertile: *able to help things grow*

germinate: *to start to grow*

harvest: *to collect as crops*

hybrid: *made by mixing two things together*

livestock: *farm animals such as chickens and cows*

Mesoamerica: *a region of southern North America that was home to ancient civilizations*

pollen: *a yellow powder made by flowers that is used to fertilize other flowers*

pollinated: *fertilized, causing seeds to grow*

shoots: *new parts that branch off from a main stem*

smut: *greasy matter caused by plant disease*

WEBSITES

Fresh for Kids: Corn
http://www.freshforkids.com.au/veg_pages/corn/corn.html
Learn fun facts about corn!

Iowa Corn: Fun for Kids
**http://www.iowacorn.org/en/corn_use_education
/fun_for_kids/**
Download corn coloring pages and activities.

Note: Every effort has been made to ensure that the websites listed above are suitable for children, that they have educational value, and that they contain no inappropriate material. However, because of the nature of the Internet, it is impossible to guarantee that these sites will remain active indefinitely or that their contents will not be altered.

READ MORE

Gibbons, Gail. *Corn.*
New York: Holiday House, 2008.

Micucci, Charles. *The Life and Times of Corn.*
Boston: Houghton Mifflin Books for Children, 2009.

32

INDEX